THE ART OF SCAMS

MIKE LOWERY

The Art of Scams

The year is 2023, and this is important. This is the reason this book came to life.

In 2023, two years after the pandemic, jobs were at an all-time low.

After receiving more money from the government then most average jobs were paying who would want to work? People were making more money staying home than they ever made working overtime.

Digital currency is now becoming heavily adopted, the BRICS alliance has been formed, the U.S. dollar is failing, real estate has fallen in value, inflation is at an all-time high, the president is falling asleep during interviews, and there are rumors that we are in a depression.

Why am I telling you this? I don't know for certain when you will pick this book up, but with no context on why I wrote it without telling you what was happening in the world. Well, it would be like a sky with no clouds.

I think it's a good time to say that this book is not to belittle anyone or any business or entity, only to tell you the truth, my truth, which may be different from your truth.

With that being said, where was I? Yes, the year is 2023, and work-from-home positions are at an all-time high. Everyone wants to work from home.

This means that more people are at home than ever, and what do they have time to do? Well, some are watching Netflix; others are on their phones, IG, and TikTok. And what are they seeing? Click the link in the bio.

I hate that phrase, but I do feel like I may use it too one day.

Algorithms have taken over social media; all day, I see credit—"Business credit," "How to get this credit card," "How to raise your credit score to 750," "How to get rich in 30 days or less," "How to make a million dollars," "Buy my course for 14.99," "Start an amazon store," "Podcast" etc.

This is my why: I was over it; I had had enough. Somebody needed to tell the truth.

Here's my truth.

Contents

CHAPTER 1

What is a scam?

The Oxford Dictionary states: a dishonest scheme, a fraud. This breaks down to deception intended to deceive others for financial gain.

This seems to be clear on paper, but what about when it's applied in real life?

Let's talk about deception: to cause someone to believe something that is not true. But what if it is true?

What if the plan or scam actually works? Is it still a scam?

Suppose two people buy a course to learn about Airbnb. One decides to take what they learn and apply it, and it is successful. They choose the right location and the right furniture and get a booking for the next weekend. Another person does the same but chooses a different location, one that is more affordable, but does not book instantly and terminates the lease after three months. Is this a scam?

The person who received the booking the very next week would tell you no, but the person who did not would tell you, yes. They would say, "I bought this course, and it was a waste of time and money." They would go on to tell you about how they had to return the furniture and pay to terminate their lease, while the other person would tell you about how they were able to open other locations and use the reviews from their clients to continue growing.

Let's pause for a minute, as we often do in life, to reflect on the person who was not successful. Why were they not successful? Was it the location? Was it that they quit too soon? Was it because they were trying to save on upfront costs?

Did they not have enough bedrooms? Maybe the furniture wasn't appealing or maybe the photos were not as good or clear?

There are millions of reasons the person was unsuccessful, but there is only one that really matters: they quit.

I became an Insurance Adjuster over seven years ago. When I first started, I didn't believe it. I was working from home—and this was before this became a thing—for a company called Sykes. I became friends with a group of girls who were in my training. We were making 14 dollars an hour, and at the time, I never made more than that. I worked other jobs at plants and 12-hour shifts that paid the same and even worked some 16-hour shifts, but to work from home and make $14.00? Well, let's say I thought I was doing pretty well.

Anyway, none of us in the group knew how to work the system. The training sucked, we didn't have an actual supervisor for about three weeks, and when we did, they didn't know what we even did. So, we would just talk. We formed a messaging group using Facebook, and we would chat or group call all day.

I was the only male in the group. So, my girlfriend hated it. One day, one of the members stated that their boyfriend got a job making $25.00 an hour.

"What"? I said. "What does he do?" She said, "We all can do it. I took his test for him."

I knew if this person could take a test and pass, I could also, but that didn't matter. "He applied to be an adjuster," she said.

"What is that?" I asked.

"I don't know," she said.

"Can you send me the info?" I asked.

And she did. I went through the orientation and watched a man cry, talking about how a company changed his life. I couldn't believe it. This was another scam. I paid to come to this course, drove my broken van for 5 hours to Atlanta with no AC, borrowed money, and dragged my girl there too.

What was I thinking? My girl was amazed; she thought this was the best thing ever and we had found a way to make more money, but I was not convinced. I felt betrayed. We left that day for the hotel, and I met a guy who told me he was an adjuster. I asked if the pay was really that good. He laughed as he pulled on the cigarette. *Great, he smokes*, I thought as I asked for a light and thought I would pick his brain as I bummed a light. I asked seriously, and he pulled out his phone and showed me a pay stub. I had been here one day, and he had been here for a week. The amount read $4,550.00.

I was sold. I had proof; I saw it. Here's a guy who made $4,550.00 in a week and had the pay stub to show it.

I was all in.

CHAPTER 2

Who Are You Talking To?

You ever had an idea that you thought was a good idea, and you decided that you wanted to do it and that it would make you a lot of money? Me too.

So, what do you do? You study, you research, and you try to find people or videos that teach you. And now you've done it. You've spent hundreds of hours on YouTube, purchasing classes and learning so much that you can't wait to tell somebody what you learned and how it's going to make you rich.

Why do we do that? Are we looking for validation? Are we trying to impress them, or are we unsure? No, we were excited and thought that maybe they would be interested and happy for us, maybe even wanted to participate.

Of course, there are those that we occasionally find are supportive and those people you should talk to only if necessary, meaning if they are not needed, don't.

We're going to focus on the other people we talk to, the ones that make you decide that maybe this isn't a good idea, maybe this will cost too much money, maybe you are not as good as you thought or this is too hard.

I told you I became an adjuster about seven years ago. The first year, I made $42,000 in one month. I was sold.

The assignment ended in December and started in November. I had made more money than I made all year in one month. In my second year, I worked for about six months. I was paid hourly on this assignment and made $8500 every two weeks. Yes, these are real numbers.

What amazed me, though, was that I was on the phone with my friend, who told me he had just bought another house and a truck and that his credit score was 800.

"How is this possible? We are both adjusters. How is that you are doing this?" I questioned. He then explained that for the past two years, he never took home less than 200k. "How?"

He said, "Well, I worked all year."

I had not worked all year, but the next year, I did. I was sitting in the car talking to my girlfriend in the hood when he called me. "What's up, man?" I said.

"Nothing man, cooling. You working?"

"Nah man, nobody call me."

"Do you want to work?" he asked.

"Hell yeah," I replied.

"Alright. I'mma have my homeboy call you."

And just like that, I was working.

I reached out to another friend who was an adjuster and told them that I did some research on Airbnb and that I was going to start this as a side hustle.

There's a guy that I grew up with who has become quite successful in doing this, and I believe it would allow me to get my time back. I could make a lot of money, have houses in different locations, and live rent-free, I explained.

My friend thought it was a good idea but started to ask me questions that were concerning: How are you going to run it? What happens if someone breaks your stuff? "I don't know, man. That might not be a good idea," he concluded.

I thought about what my friend said and became hesitant, so I called my successful Airbnb friend. We had not spoken for years. I actually inboxed him. *"Hey man, I'm interested in doing this, but I don't want to gamble. Is it possible that I could buy one of your locations that have already been successful?"*

He called me. "What's up, man? How you been, bro?"

"Good," I replied. "I'm really interested in doing this, man."

He said, "Ok, I got your message. I don't really do this bro, but I'll do it for you. I will give you one of my locations."

"How much?" I eagerly asked.

He said, "I'm going to have to charge you twenty thousand."

Whoa, that's all I had in my savings. "Twenty?" I said, not wanting to sound like I didn't have it,

"Yeah. Think about it and let me know," he said.

"Ok, cool man. I appreciate it," I concluded.

I called my other friend from earlier, who was concerned. "Hey man, I just talked to…, and he said I could get one of his for twenty. That way I don't take no risk."

My concerned friend immediately came with more doubt. "Twenty? Man, twenty, that's a lot. Are you sure the Airbnb is doing numbers?"

"Yeah," I said. "He said he would send all the paperwork and change the log information."

"I don't know, man," my friend said. "I wouldn't do it."

"I'mma think about it," I said as I got off the phone. "Fuck," I said. I really hadn't talked to my Airbnb friend in a long time. *People do change*, I said to myself. *Maybe he's right. Maybe I should just keep my money. That is a lot to lose.*

In both experiences, I talked to different friends. When I wanted to make more money as an adjuster, I simply talked to someone who did, and it became my truth.

I wanted to own an Airbnb, but I talked to one person who was successful in Airbnb and the other who never owned an Airbnb. I let my friend, who never owned an Airbnb, put doubt and fear into what I wanted to do. Now, the hours and research seemed like kindergarten information and that I needed to go to college. I also talked to my Airbnb friend, who had nothing but positive things to say about it. Was it a scam?

Or did I miss out on becoming successful with Airbnb because I was scared?

CHAPTER 3

The Art of Scams Middlemen

Several platforms have become outlets to obtain entrepreneurship.

At least, that is what most people think. A few of these are Airbnb, Turo, stocks, credit repair companies, YouTube, and TikTok.

What do all of these have in common?

Most people would say, "I'm an entrepreneur," "I have a YouTube channel," "I am an entrepreneur," "I have a Turo business," etc. While these people say they are entrepreneurs, they are not. This is a lie that has been perceived as truth.

They are not entrepreneurs; they are workers, and though the pay structure is different, they do not set their payment.

As an adjuster, even though my pay increased, I did not set my own pay rate; someone still paid me—the company I worked for. I believed that since I set my own appointment times, I was my own boss. This is where I was wrong. Yes, I did set my appointment times. Yes, I did drive my own car. Yes, I did decide if I wanted to work late or early. However, the company penalized me for not completing assignments or turning in inspection notes or estimates within a certain time frame.

As these companies allow flexibility, they do not qualify as entrepreneurship.

You must follow all guidelines when uploading to YouTube, and you do not set your pay rate. After so many clicks or likes will you get a check or so many subscribers. The same goes for TikTok and Instagram.

You may put more cars on Turo, but you still work for Turo. You can set your prices, but you must be competitive, or your car will probably not get booked.

These are workers working for middlemen. Who is a middleman? Well, if you ever bought weed or any illegal drug, you got it from a middleman. Even when you thought you got it from the plug, you didn't. How do I know? Well, I don't. But if you could call your weed guy and have him pull up or go to him the same day, he's a middleman.

We often think because someone has a lot, they are the plug. No, they simply have a lot, which means they owe a lot or paid a lot— cheaper to buy in bulk.

For those that don't understand, when you go grocery shopping at Sam's instead of Walmart, you go for the bulk items. The items are more in quantity, not more in value. Therefore, Sam's is the middleman. Sam's is not the source; the plug is. There are several middlemen over middlemen over middlemen.

CHAPTER 4

Worker Vs Entrepreneur

There is nothing wrong with workers, but it should be clear that they are not entrepreneurs.

Workers work. Simply put, if they don't work, they don't eat.

Turo is a platform where individuals lease their cars. I started doing this about two years ago. It was great that I made money by simply renting my car out, right? No.

I had two cars, and I had to keep them washed, cleaned, gas, and delivered. This was a job. I then delegated the task of washing and keeping the cars clean to my father-in-law. He and my girlfriend would deliver the cars to the airport and other places when needed. Was I an entrepreneur now? No, I still worked for Turo, and if I canceled a trip, it dropped my performance, which meant fewer bookings and a lower payout. I was working to create more work, believing the lie that I was working to create freedom.

A hairstylist who did my hair in LA had just sprung her ankle. She had many hustles, but this one in particular was unique. She was a hairstylist who moved from North Carolina to LA and started doing hair. I asked why she would take such a big risk, and she simply stated there was room to grow.

Many stylists have done my hair, and they basically have the same rules: they charge a fee, and if you are late, they charge an additional fee. They usually make you pay a deposit.

This hair stylist did something different with her business. She had a two-for-one deal, meaning you pay for one, and you can get another one for free the same month. I thought to myself, *This is a great idea*, and then I said, "That's got to be exhausting. Do people take you up on this deal?"

She replied, "Yes, everyone I do gets the deal, but some don't make it back within the month." Wow, she was building retention, guaranteeing repetitive customers more work to create more work. Is this an entrepreneur? No, she is still working in the booth and has to pay rent. She may make more than everyone else, but she is not an entrepreneur. Or is she?

This stylist, who is a good friend, and I recommend you all to go to her, started doing customers overseas. What about now? Is she an entrepreneur? Now that she is an international hairstylist, is she an entrepreneur? No. Or is she?

No, she is a worker creating a lane for entrepreneurship. What does that mean? Well, she opened her own salon and hired a stylist who now works for her. Now, is she an entrepreneur? Yes, this is her business.

While I was learning how to make more money on Turo, about the insurance programs, and trying to keep my cars safe, I met a guy while dropping off my car at the airport.

He had 14 cars, and they all remained at the airport. He had hired someone to come out and detail the cars and gas them up, and the customer could only pick them up and drop them at the airport. Is he an entrepreneur? I asked how he did it, how he kept up with 14 cars, and he said it was exhausting. He still had to be a part of the system—when a car did not get dropped off, answering emails. He was still working. He had scaled his business by adding cars, yet adding more work.

I had learned that if I had more certification and classes to add to my resume, I would have a more marketable resume, which would lead to more and higher paying jobs. More work to create more work.

Credit repair companies are of two kinds: one where the person actually reviews your credit and submits letters on your behalf accordingly, and another where AI is used to submit letters randomly, and there is no one actually reading and discussing with you what they are actually doing in those 90 days, only that dispute letters have been sent.

One is entrepreneurship, and the other is work.

CHAPTER 5

Who Is an entrepreneur, aka The Inventor?

Oxford Definition: a person who organizes a business or business, taking on greater than normal financial risk in order to do so.

Well, that's weird. I thought the definition meant someone who starts a business from nothing or creates ways of getting passive income. That sounds more like someone who unfucks a fucked up situation. Why would anybody want to do that? Why would anybody want to organize a business clearly if it needs organizing? It's a mess, and you take on financial risk, meaning you could lose money. I'm good on that. I need to change my IG page now.

Why do we glorify this bullshit? Oh yeah, I forgot we believed a lie that was told and said so much it became the truth.

Wait, here's the right definition: an individual who starts their own business based on an idea they have or a product they have created while assuming most of the risk and reaping most of the rewards of the business.

That's better.

So basically, I have to start a business based on something I created and assume the responsibility of marketing and selling it. So, how the fuck could a Turo host be an entrepreneur? How the fuck could a YouTuber be an entrepreneur?

In other words, the entrepreneur invents.

The inventor... I thought about keeping this chapter out. I knew that this would be a topic that people would probably not like, but out of all, I feel this is the most necessary to complete this book.

The inventor... When we think of the word "inventor," we automatically think of invention and that we must invent something, and unless

20

you're like Elon Musk or Bill Gates, well, this can get pretty hard to do, isn't it?

Let's talk about my friend, the hairstylist—excuse me, international hair stylist sounds better—who moved from her hometown to grow. This was the first move. She was in control. She then got a job working in a salon. "Where are you going with this?" Follow me. She then began training, paid training. Not training on being a loctician; training on running a business. Do you see? Yes, she had client's she was working with, but unlike most people, she wasn't working to create work; she was working to create freedom. She eventually bought her own salon and sold a product for locs that she made. Two for one. She owns the salon, has others working for her, and sells a product only she can supply.

Let's take, for example, my friend with the 14 cars. He had detailers and many other workers apart of his Turo business, which is important. Turo business, not his. He paid them, supervised them, and created another job, more work.

Now let's talk about my other friend who had a car rental business. Did you notice the difference? It's his. He had started on Turo also, using the same platform and knowledge. He also had workers. The major thing that the stylist and my two Turo friends had in common was that they started a system. They invented one. This is key. The system operated on Turo, yes, but one of my friends transferred the knowledge he gained at Turo and the cars he had obtained to his own brand. Now, there is no cap on the amount he can make. He charges his own price with the same system he developed at Turo. The same goes for the stylist; she transferred the knowledge she gained from working at a salon to owning a salon.

What are you saying, invent? Inventing does not have to be something that's never been seen or didn't exist. Just recreate. One of my favorite sayings is, "You don't have to reinvent the wheel." An invention could be a song, a melody, a product, a business, or a system, but you must apply the system to your business.

CHAPTER 6

The Game Is to Be Sold, Not to Be Told

This is a quote I heard Snoop Dog say when I was a child.

It was also repeated by a lot of the older drug dealers in my neighborhood What did it mean?

Information is key. Have you ever heard that phrase before? When you purchase an e-book or a course, a how to lesson, you are buying the information. When you work your ass off to get a scholarship or have rich parents that pay for you to go to the best colleges, you pay tuition. The same fucking thing. Are you saying that college is a scam? Well, let me ask you a question. Did you pay for a course to learn. Well, then I let you be the judge. Remember, it's only a scam if it is not true.

The point is information is for sale. Whew, that was a mouthful. I'mma say it again: Information is for sale. You buy the information to obtain it, then it is a matter of applying what you have learned. This is why the E-commerce business has boomed so much in 2023. Everyone is at home learning and learning and learning.

Some have chosen to apply the information, learn from the mistakes that they made, and continue to move forward, one step in front of the other. You don't need to know every answer but just how to take the next step. By doing this, you are moving forward.

What does this mean? If I give you the answers to a test, have you passed? No, you haven't taken the test.

What about a cheat sheet? No, you haven't taken the test. Not until you've taken the test do you pass.

But beware of outdated information; here's one of my favorite I hear all the time.

If you apply for a Navy Federal credit card after 2:00 am, you'll automatically get a high limit because no one is there, and the computer will automatically approve you, or the complete opposite; it'll get sent to underwriting, and a real person will get it, and they're likely to approve it. Why this may have been true 10 years ago, why would you believe this? This sounds completely stupid. What in this sentence would make someone believe this dumb shit? Oh yeah, I forgot: hearing it over and over until it's perceived to be true.

This is why so many credit gurus say the same shit; they heard it, and they told someone, and they told someone else, and now it's millions of videos all over YouTube saying the same bull shit.

Validate your information.

Here's the easy way to get the credit card. Ask someone who has the fucking card how they got it, and make sure they tell you how they got it.

I apply this to everything in life. If you want the Rolls Royce, ask someone with a Rolls Royce how they got it.

You want an 800 credit score? Ask someone with an 800.

I was in the Army, so people who want to join the military always ask how the military is, and my reply is the same.

I can't tell you about the military. There are four different sections: Navy, Airforce, Marines, Army, and I think they have a space force now. So weird, right? We actually have a space force. I know I met a group of soldiers who actually were in the space force. Anyhow, I can only tell you about the Army when I was in it. I cannot speak for the Navy because I have never been on a ship, nor can I tell you what's life like in the Air Force because I wasn't in it. I apply this to everything in life. If you wanted to learn how to swim, would you ask a fish or bird? You would ask the fish, so why do we listen to birds as if they have swam before? It's the same. If I want to know how to fly, I'll ask a bird, not a fish. What can it tell me about flying? How it seems dangerous?

I take this further. If I want to fly, I don't just ask any bird; I ask the bird I want to be like—the eagle, because nothing flies higher than an eagle but an eagle.

I ask the best. If I want to be it, I ask the best. If I can't find the best, I research the best.

Information is key, but validated information coming from the right source is everything.

Notice how I said I can tell you about the Army when I was in there but I cannot tell you about it now.

Information changes just like the Army. Nothing stays the same. It is imperative to verify that the information is up to date. Your source needs to be up to date.

Made in the USA
Columbia, SC
13 March 2024

32665070R00021